WELCOME TO THE WORLD OF
Owls

Diane Swanson

Whitecap Books
Vancouver / Toronto

The information in this book is true and complete to the best of our knowledge.
All recommendations are made without guarantee on the part of the author or
Whitecap Books. The author and publisher disclaim any liability in connection
with the use of this information. For additional information please contact
Whitecap Books, 351 Lynn Avenue, North Vancouver, BC V7J 2C4.

Edited by Elizabeth McLean
Cover design by Steve Penner
Cover photograph by Joe MacDonald/First Light
Interior design by Margaret Ng
Typeset by Tanya Lloyd
Photo credits: Thomas Kitchin/First Light iv, 2, 6, 14; Robert Lankinen/First
Light 4; Michio Hoshino/First Light 8; Victoria Hurst/First Light 10; Brian
Milne/First Light 12; Joe MacDonald/First Light 16; Jim Zuckerman/First Light
18; Darwin Wiggett/First Light 20; Steve Bentsen/First Light 22; Chase
Swift/First Light 24; Jim Brandenburg/First Light 26

Printed and bound in Canada

Canadian Cataloguing in Publication Data

Swanson, Diane, 1944–
    Welcome to the world of owls

    Includes index.
    ISBN 1-55110-614-0

    1. Owls—Juvenile literature. I. Title.
QL696.S8S92 1997   j598.9'7   C97-910656-7

For more information on
this series and other
Whitecap Books titles,
visit our web site at
www.whitecap.ca

The publisher acknowledges the support of the Canada Council for the Arts for
our publishing program and the Cultural Services Branch of the Government of
British Columbia in making this publication possible.

Contents

World of Difference

WHAT A SHARP BIRD THE OWL IS. It has a sharp, curved beak. It has sharp, hooked claws—called talons. It even has super sharp senses.

The owl can hear much better than most other animals can. Feathers hide the big ears on the sides of its head. But these ears are so keen they can hear beetles rustling in grass. The ears are not quite level with each other, which helps them pinpoint sound.

The owl has amazing sight, too. Unlike most birds, it looks out from big eyes in the front of its head. Staring with both eyes at once helps the owl judge how large—and

Day and night, the great gray owl sees very well. Its huge head makes its large eyes seem small.

1

how far away—something is. Even at night, the owl sees well. Its eyes take in a lot more light than yours do.

One thing the owl can't do is move its eyes much. If it wants to see side to side, it turns its whole head. Its neck is so well built for turning that the owl can even see what's right behind it.

Snuggled in its thick coat, the snowy owl stays warm—even on snow.

Around the world, there are more than 130 different kinds of owls. In North America, there are nearly 20, and they come in all sizes. The three biggest are the great horned owl, the great gray owl, and the snowy owl. If any of these owls stood on a piano, its wing tips would touch both ends at once. But the wings of the elf owl spread only one-fifth that far. Weighing less than a small bar of hand soap, it is the tiniest owl in North America.

ALL-WEATHER FEATHER COATS

Owls wear thick, all-weather coats made of thousands of feathers. Short feathers keep out extreme heat and cold. Long feathers keep out rain. In North America, the snowy owl wears the thickest owl coat of all. It even covers its legs and feet.

Owls that fly at night have special coats. Fluffy fringes on their flight feathers muffle the noise of rushing air. That's how owls can swoop after prey without making a sound.

Where in the World

DIFFERENT OWLS NEED DIFFERENT HOMES. Some owls live in dark, damp forests of old trees. Others choose sunny, dry fields or hot, sandy deserts. There are owls on high mountains and owls in deep canyons; owls near swamps, inside caves, and underground. Some even hang around cities and farms, resting on buildings and fenceposts.

Most owls have home territories—areas where they hunt. Little owls have little territories; big owls have big ones. A pair of great horned owls might have a territory as large as 13 square kilometres (5 square

Quiet, dark woods attract the barred owl. It often perches close to a tree trunk.

5

If they feel safe, barn owls may stay in a barn even when people are working nearby.

miles). That's the size of some ranches. But if there's plenty of food, owls use smaller territories than usual.

When the weather turns cold, many owls stay put. Others head to warmer places for the winter. They may just move down a mountain, or fly to another country. Snowy owls from the Arctic often spend winter in southern Canada or the northern United States. In bitter winters when food is very scarce, they fly as far as Bermuda and India.

Except for Antarctica, every continent is home to owls of one kind or another. The most common owl in North America is the great horned owl. It lives in many different types of homes. But some kinds of owls need special places. Spotted owls, for instance, live in old forests, so there are fewer of these owls now than there once were.

HAUNTED HOUSE OWLS

It's a dark night. You hear a frightening howl. Something white swoops through an empty house and out a broken window. As ghostly as it seems, it's only a barn owl, heading off on a hunt.

Barn owls live in dark corners of empty houses, barns, church towers, and bridges. They hunt the many mice that live on farms, in parks, down back alleys, and along train tracks. But the sights and sounds of barn owls trigger many stories of ghosts and haunted houses.

7

World of the Hunter

WHEN OWLS HUNT, THEY USE GOOD SENSE. They watch carefully for their prey. They listen closely. Then they strike.

The small boreal owl uses a low branch in the forest as a lookout. When it senses prey, it turns and lowers its head to pinpoint the sound, then takes off. During the last stretch, it glides smoothly as it brings its feet forward and pounces.

Sometimes a great gray owl hears an animal, perhaps a mouse, moving under the snow. The owl swoops after it, hovers briefly over the sound, then

Hunting to feed its family keeps this snowy owl busy.

9

Mostly a day-time hunter, the northern hawk-owl has captured dinner — a deer mouse.

dives. As its head plunges into the snow, its long legs shoot forward. Toes and talons nab the prey.

The needle-sharp talons on an owl's grasping toes are powerful hunting tools. Two of the toes on each foot point forward and one points back. Depending on how the owl wants to use its feet, it can turn its fourth toe to the front, side, or back. Holding two toes forward and two back helps the owl clutch and carry heavy prey.

Some owls—such as elf owls—hunt during the day, but most hunt at night. Usually, big owls eat big prey; small owls eat small prey. They feed mainly on furry animals, such as mice, rats, moles, squirrels, rabbits— even skunks. They also eat insects, spiders, frogs, and small birds. In the world of the hunter, owls eat well.

PELLETS OF PLENTY

GULP! Owls often swallow small prey whole. They store unwanted pieces, such as teeth, claws, and fur, in the gizzard—part of their stomach. Strong muscles roll them into small balls called pellets. Then the owl coughs them up.

Scientists poke through pellets to learn what owls eat. They may find the skull of a mouse, the leg of a beetle—even the scales of a fish. They compare pellets to see how seasons change what owls eat.

World of Words

OWLS ARE JUST LIKE PEOPLE: Some talk a lot; some talk a little. But when owls get angry, most snap their beaks or click their tongues and hiss-s-s.

Owls make different sounds for different reasons. They "talk" to claim their territories, warn their enemies, court their mates, and call to other owls—including their young.

For example, a male barn owl courts a female by chanting "whee-tuh…whee-tuh…whee-tuh…" A female spotted owl whistles softly as she comes to her nest or leaves it. Two barred owls in trees call

A young short-eared owl hisses and snaps its beak, trying to scare what threatens it.

Tufts of head feathers move up and down, forward and backward to help this screech owl "talk."

loudly to each other: HOO-HOO-HOO-HOO-HOO-HOO-HOO-HOO.

In fact, barred owls are the chattiest owls in North America. They talk day and night, using screams, cries, hoots, shrieks, trills, squeals, grumbles, and barks.

Big owls usually have deeper voices than small owls do. But one small owl—the flammulated owl—has a very low-pitched voice. That makes the owl sound bigger than it really is. Still, when the flammulated owl is frightened, it meows like a kitten.

Some owls, such as great horned owls and screech owls, have tufts of feathers on the tops of their heads. The tufts look like ears, but they help owls talk—not hear. Poked up and forward, the tufts mean: "Stay out of my territory." Pressed down and back, they say: "Aw, be nice."

HOOTS THAT SPOOK

For centuries, people around the world believed that hooting owls brought bad luck. Hunters gave up hunting if an owl on their left side hooted three times. Parents thought their babies would have trouble if owls hooted at the birth.

Some people linked hooting with sickness, such as tonsillitis. Others believed hoots meant someone would die. They tried to prevent the death by throwing salt into fire.

15

World of Mates

MANY OWLS HAVE A LIFETIME
MATE—one they win through courting.
And when owls go courting, they do it
with style.

Some kinds take to the skies. The male
short-eared owl circles his territory to say
he's available, then puts on a show. Sometimes he climbs high, hovers in the wind,
and sings. Then he glides, claps his wings
under his body, and climbs up again. For a
grand finish, he zooms down, rocking his
body side to side.

Then the short-eared owl may grab
some prey and land. If he has attracted a

This screech
owl is winging
its way home.
It nests with
its mate in the
hollow of a tree.

female, she flies to him. He flutters his wings and presents her with dinner.

Some owls depend more on their voices to court. Male and female screech owls bond by singing duets. Pairs of great horned owls hoot while bowing. When they hoot a long time, they often rub beaks, too. And among great gray owls, the male hums as he rubs his beak

"Hey, I'm SQUISHED!"
These three great horned owl siblings are crowded into a nest built by a hawk.

against a female. Then he combs her feathers, and she combs his.

Few owls build nests to receive their eggs. Some look for old bird nests, tree holes, or nooks among rocks. Burrowing owls choose underground tunnels. The male prepares the tunnel and sings to a female near the entrance. They might nibble each other's feathers. Then he hunts for food to give her. After dinner, the singing, nibbling, and hunting may start all over again.

HOW OWLS WOW

Nesting owls often surprise people. Here's how:

- Elf owls nest only in holes made by wood-peckers — some in trees, some in cacti.
- When there's plenty of food, snowy owls may lay 10 eggs at a time. But when food is scarce, they may not lay any.
- Burrowing owls add animal droppings to their underground nests. That makes it harder for enemies to smell the owls.

19

New World

YOUNG OWLS TAKE THEIR TIME GROWING UP. So parents, such as great horned owls, start nesting in winter. Their eggs take up to 35 days to hatch. All that time, the mother owl warms the eggs with her body, turning them with her beak and feet.

When they hatch, young owls—called owlets—don't even open their eyes for days. Their mother keeps them tucked safely beneath her. As the owlets grow, she rests close beside them, sometimes hiding them under her wings.

Father owls catch and bring prey to the

To defend its young, the great horned owl attacks any intruder fiercely.

nest. As hungry as owlets always are, they rarely try to grab each other's food. In fact, the owlets that hatched first may help feed the younger ones.

When owlets grow bigger, they stay alone while both their parents hunt. But if enemies, such as hawks, threaten the nest, the parents zoom back to

If they're not bothered, barn owls often use the same nest time after time. They may live 5 to 11 years.

attack. Owls dive and slash at anything that threatens their young.

Until they can fly, owlets that hatch in holes—such as elf owlets—usually stay tucked inside. Those that hatch in ground nests, such as snowy owlets, pop in and out. And tree-nesters, such as barred owlets, scramble over branches—even climbing the trees—before they can fly.

It may be fall by the time young owls can find food on their own. Then they're ready to explore the bigger world.

FEATHERED FUN

Owls play with their food before eating. They shake their prey and tear it. They toss it and pounce on it. Caged owls also play with things they can't eat, such as wads of paper.

Some owls play with each other. Barn owls play together by pushing and wrestling owl-style. Like other animals, they play most when they're young. Playing helps owls exercise and grow strong. It also teaches them to watch closely and react fast.

23

Tricky World

OWLS ARE A HOOT! They play tricks to escape danger. They may "disappear" by blending with their backgrounds. The long-eared owl is especially good at this. It presses itself close to a tree trunk that matches its brownish feathers. Then it pushes its feathery "moustache" forward to hide its beak. Sometimes it also shuts its eyes. Even if you're close to a long-eared owl, it's very hard to spot.

Owls also make themselves look bigger and tougher than they are. It's a useful trick to play on animals that threaten them or their nests. Fluffing out their feathers makes

The saw-whet owl can hide from bigger owls by blending in with a tree trunk.

25

When they go underground, young burrowing owls imitate the sounds of rattlesnakes to scare away enemies.

owls seem twice as big. And spreading their large wings makes them look even bigger. Then the owls clack their beaks and hiss. Some also sway side to side to look extra tough.

Playing dead is another trick used by owls, such as snowy and barn owls. Then their enemies usually leave them alone.

Some grown owls, such as the short-eared, pretend to be injured, not dead. That's how they lead enemies, including people, away from their owlets. Then the owls fly off to safety.

Many owls trick enemies by "throwing" their voices, making their calls seem to come from someplace else. The saw-whet owl, for example, has fooled people into thinking a different owl was calling from a tree behind them—when it was actually in front of them.

OWLS THAT RATTLE

In their tunnels, burrowing owls make a sound like a rattlesnake rattling its tail. That scares skunks and coyotes, which eat owls. It also scares ground squirrels that might try to move in.

Scientists put a tape recorder in a tunnel to play the sounds of rattlesnakes and burrowing owls. The owl sounds scared the ground squirrel as much as the snake sounds. Its teeth chattered. Its tail hair stood on end. And the ground squirrel ran away.

Index